The West of Ireland
A Megalithic Primer

Helen F. North   Mary C. North

Iona Foundation
Philadelphia, Pennsylvania

Iona Foundation, Columban Celtic Series, Volume 3
P.O. Box 29136
Philadelphia, PA 19127

Photographs: Virginia F. Babcock and the authors
Book Design: Audree Penner

Printed by XYAN Inc. in the United States of America

Library of Congress Cataloging-in-Publication Data
North, Helen F. (Helen Florence), 1921–
    The West of Ireland : a megalithic primer / Helen F. North, Mary C.
North : photographs, Virginia F. Babcock and the authors.
        p. cm. — (Columban Celtic series : v. 3)
    Includes bibliographical references.
    ISBN 0-941638-03-0 (pbk. : alk. paper)
    1. Megalithic monuments—Ireland Guidebooks. 2. Ireland
–Antiquities Guidebooks. 3. Ireland Guidebooks. I. North, Mary C. (Mary
Carol), 1919–   . II. Title. III. Series.
GN806.5.N67   1999
914. 1704'824—dc21
                                                99-40741CIP

Cover photograph: Coom Wedge Grave, County Kerry

In Memoriam

Virginia F. Babcock
Helen M. McCann

For support and counsel of various kinds, the authors wish to
thank John F. Callahan, Daniel J. Gillis, Vartan Gregorian,
Tom and Lynn Mitchell, Bob Wood and all the people in the West of
Ireland who have answered our questions and helped us on our way.

Assistance from a private donor is gratefully acknowledged.

Introduction

Ireland is blessed with about 1500 prehistoric structures called megaliths, from Greek *megas* (big) and *lithos* (stone), most of them tombs. This guidebook aims to help visitors locate some forty such monuments that are rewarding to visit, but not as well known and well signposted as those famous landmarks, the Newgrange tumulus in County Meath and the Poulnabrone dolmen in County Clare.

Our examples range from very accessible to exceptionally well hidden, and they include specimens of all four principal varieties of megalithic tomb, plus a sampling of stone circles, alignments, and standing stones.

Dating: All dates are approximate. According to current consensus Ireland's first inhabitants arrived during the Mesolithic (Middle Stone) Age, c. 7500 B.C. The Neolithic (New Stone) Age, in which agriculture began (c. 3500 B.C.), probably saw the earliest megalithic building. The Bronze Age in Ireland began c. 2100 B.C. and the Iron Age c. 700 B.C. Only in the Iron Age did the Celts appear; hence it is impossible for their priestly caste, the Druids, to have built the megaliths, any more than they built Stonehenge.

The tombs built by inhabitants of Ireland beginning in Neolithic times are conventionally assigned to four major groups: **court cairns, portal tombs or dolmens, passage graves, and wedge-shaped gallery graves**. The word "dolmen" derives from two Breton words: *dol* (table) and *men* (stone). The second of these terms, combined with Breton *hir* (tall), appears also in the word "menhir," tall stone, applied to standing stones, in Irish "gallán." Another word often encountered in the older literature, "cromlech," comes from Irish *crom* (curved) and *leac* (stone). Because it was used with a variety of meanings (portal tomb, stone circle), it is now avoided as potentially confusing.

Court cairns, the earliest type, of which almost 400 have been identified, but only 38 excavated, are mostly North of a line drawn from Galway to Dundalk. They are characterized by an open, rounded forecourt leading to a flat-roofed gallery covered by a mound, often trapezoidal. The gallery, which is the burial chamber, is usually subdivided into two to four chambers by upright jambs in the side walls. Burials are multiple, usually cremations. Some court cairns have the court in the center, others two courts at opposite ends. Typically court cairns have the entrance on the East. Some kind of ritual may have been celebrated in the court, and burial may not have been the only or principal function. Court cairns are not grouped in cemeteries. In regions where several are known (as around Buntrahir Bay in Mayo, where 28 such tombs have been found) they average three miles apart, as if each served as a center - political, religious or both - for a family or clan. They are thought to date from the middle of the fourth millennium (3500 B.C. and thereafter) and are older than the pyramids of Giza and the beehive tombs of Mycenae, as well as Stonehenge. The long barrows of Britain are comparable in certain ways to Irish court cairns.

Portal dolmens, popularly known as Druids' Altars or Dermot and Grania's Beds, may be contemporary with the court cairns, to which they have certain affinities in structure and location. They are the most dramatic of Irish megaliths, being above ground, constructed of two uprights (orthostats) forming the portal (often facing East) and one or more other uprights, lower than the portal stones, supporting one or sometimes two huge capstones that slant towards the rear of the chamber. Some show traces of a cairn, which may not, however, have completely covered them. Some may have had courts in front of the portal; some had an extra chamber at the rear. About 160 portal dolmens exist, mostly in the North and Northwest, but with a scattering on the East coast, mainly between Dublin and Waterford. Only a few have been excavated, sometimes revealing cremation burials.

Passage graves consist of a burial chamber entered by a long, narrow passage, both covered by a mound, usually surrounded by stone curbing and sometimes adorned inside and out with stones decorated with geometric motifs. The burial chamber may be round, polygonal, or cruciform. Cremated remains have been found, occasionally on or near a stone basin within the burial chamber. About 230 passage graves are known, varying greatly in size and orientation, and only a few have been excavated. They are often grouped in cemeteries in prominent positions on hilltops or ridges, where smaller, satellite tombs cluster around a very large specimen. This is especially true of the great cemeteries distributed between the Boyne Valley and Sligo Bay. Other examples, in Ulster and Leinster, tend to be more isolated. In areas where passage tombs and the slightly earlier court cairns coexist, they sometimes share structural characteristics.

Wedge-shaped gallery graves, of which almost 500 are known, are found mostly to the West of a North-South line running from Derry to Cork. They consist of a long, narrow burial chamber defined by upright stones, sometimes in a double row, often tapering towards the rear (hence the name "wedge-shaped"). The stones at the entrance tend to be taller, so that the capstones slant downward towards the rear. Some examples have a second chamber at the front or back. The entrance usually faces Southwest. Cremation burials, sometimes single, have been found. Many wedge tombs exist in areas (such as the Burren, Co. Clare) associated with grazing, but others are near ancient copper mines (e.g., in West Cork). Constructed near the beginning of the third millennium B.C., wedge tombs were used well into the second. Breton gallery graves (late Neolithic) are somewhat similar to the Irish variety, but without the characteristic wedge shape.

Other megalithic structures

Standing stones (menhirs, gALLáns) occur throughout Ireland and were probably erected at different times for a variety of reasons - to mark burials, to indicate boundaries, possibly to serve as cult objects. They range in time from the Bronze Age to the early Christian era. There is an unbroken sequence of such monuments from prehistoric times to the age of the High Crosses (late ninth century to c. 1200 A.D.), which are the final and most elaborate stage of the Irish stone-cult. Particularly interesting are standing stones of pre-Christian origin that have been baptized by the carving of a cross (or other Christian symbol) on the front of the slab.

A late (not properly megalithic or prehistoric) subdivision of the standing stone category is the **ogham stone,** inscribed along one edge with marks derived from the Roman alphabet, usually recording a proper name and probably serving as a memorial. The earliest specimens go back to the fourth or fifth century after Christ and pre-serve the earliest method of writing in Irish, a method that continued in use for centuries. Ogham stones are scattered throughout Ireland, but exist in greatest numbers in Cork and Kerry, often in monastic settings. They are also found in the West of Britain, especially Wales. The name ogham recalls the god Ogmios, the inventor of writing in the Celtic pantheon.

Alignments (rows of standing stones) are rare and short compared to the impressive specimens in Brittany and Avebury, but some exist on high ground, especially in Kerry and Cork, where seven is the maximum number of stones.

Stone circles. Circles (or approximately circular groupings) of standing stones, often with "outliers," are numerous, especially in Kerry and Cork. Not primarily associated with burials, they are often thought to have had a ritual or astronomical purpose because of the orientation of particular stones so that between or above them a significant, recurring astronomical event may readily be sighted. Dating is difficult, but many circles are considered to belong to the Bronze Age (beginning c. 2100 B.C.).

Most of the megalithic and other monuments described here stand on private property. Signposts (far less numerous than twenty years ago and often defaced when they do exist) do not indicate state ownership. Visitors should always take care to close gates and otherwise respect the rights of owners, most of whom - but not all - are inclined to be helpful. One motive for writing this guidebook is to encourage visitors who will, by their interest in Ireland's prehistoric treasures, contribute to the effort to preserve them.

Glossary:
Alignment: row of standing stones.
Capstone: roofstone.
Corbelling: roofing by overlapping stones.
Cupmark: round depression, sometimes surrounded by circles.
Cairn: mound, generally of stone, sometimes of turf, covering a tomb.
Center-court tomb: court cairn having court in center with galleries on either side.
Double-court tomb: court cairn with two tombs back to back.
Full-court tomb: court cairn with forecourt consisting of full circle.

Jambstones: upright stones on either side of entrance or of chamber within tomb.

Orthostat: upright stone.

Septal slab: stone slab dividing chamber or passage.

Arrangement of this guidebook: The eight counties treated are listed in alphabetical order: **Clare, Donegal, Galway, Kerry, Limerick, Mayo, Roscommon, Sligo**. Within counties monuments are alphabetical, except when proximity of two sites makes it advisable to list them together.

Further Reading:

We are profoundly indebted to two priceless books now out of print:

E. Estyn Evans, *Prehistoric and Early Christian Ireland: A Guide,* London, 1966.

Anthony Weir, *Early Ireland: A Field Guide,* Belfast, 1980.

The following is a very select list of especially helpful books in print:

Peter Harbison, *Ancient Irish Monuments*, Dublin,1997.

    Guide to the National and Historic Monuments of Ireland, Dublin, 1993.

    Pre-Christian Ireland From the First Settlers to the Early Celts, London, 1988.

Kenneth McNally, *Standing Stones and Other Monuments of Early Ireland,* Belfast, 1984.

Elizabeth Shee Twohig, *Irish Megalithic Tombs*, Princes Risborough, 1990.

Local guidebooks are recommended in connection with specific sites. Also mentioned are other, neighboring monuments, not necessarily megalithic, worthy of a visit. In the case of sites that are especially difficult to locate, it is advisable to consult local informants, preferably elderly. Post office personnel are usually knowledgeable.

Some acquaintance with the Irish roots from which place names come will be helpful. P.W. Joyce, *Irish Local Names Explained* (Dublin, 1968) is a convenient handbook.

County Clare

County Clare is the home of a special, very simple, box-like variety of wedge-shaped gallery grave made of the large, rectangular slabs abundant in the Burren, the spectacular limestone plateau of NW Clare, overlooking Galway Bay. Two very useful guidebooks are Burren Journey *(1978) and* Burren Journey West *(1980), both by* George Cunningham. Indispensable is the map of the Burren by T.D. Robinson. All three are available in offices of the Irish Tourist Board. Well worth visiting also are the 12th-century High Crosses at Kilfenora, the monastic site of Dysart O'Dea, and the substantial ruins of Corcomroe Abbey.

Gleninsheen Wedge Grave. About 4 miles S of Ballyvaughan on road to Leamaneh Castle, 1 mile N of the portal dolmen of Poulnabrone, signposted, to the E of the road and close to it. A small, neat, typical Burren wedge grave with the usual large capstone, supported by two large sidestones. The W end is closed by two stones, and just beyond it, towards the road, a large stony mound may be the remains of a cairn.

Baur South Wedge Grave. Almost a mile S of Gleninsheen and 5 miles SW of Ballyvaughan (shortly before Poulnabrone) a byroad to the W leads to Baur South, where lurks one of the best-hidden and most interesting wedge graves in the Burren. About a mile in from the Ballyvaughan-Leamaneh road is the end of a lane leading (N) to Mr. Healy's dairy farm. Continue W on the byroad about 400 meters to a point where the roadside wall meets a second wall at an angle. The second wall is intersected by a third wall (roughly at right angles), and the wedge grave is in the angle between these two walls. Its unusual feature is a chamber within the main chamber, sharing the same backstone. The roofstone supports a growth of turf that makes it hard to see the tomb among the surrounding brambles, and the lack of any notable landmarks as you look N from the road makes this the hardest of the Burren wedge graves to detect.

Parknabinnia Wedge Graves. Three wedge graves can be visited with relative ease along a byroad leading from Kilnaboy towards Cloncoose, one of several leading off the Corofin-Kilfenora road along the S edge of the Burren.

Parknabinnia I. If travelling W from Corofin, ignore the first byroad (signposted for Boston) and turn right (N) at the second. The road is very narrow and has many sharp turns as it climbs steeply uphill to the crest of the Burren. About 1³/₁₀ miles N of Kilnaboy a signpost to the left (W) of the road (**Leaba: Wedge Tomb**) points over a stile to the tomb, which is close to the road and parallel to it. Large, single slabs form the two sides; the roofstone, about ten feet long, is covered with turf and bog asphodel; a door-

stone practically covers the entrance , and the chamber is almost completely closed at the opposite end. Many stones (from the cairn?) lie scattered behind the tomb. Just across the road stands another signpost, now bereft of its original sign, which once read Viewing Point, East Burren. A short walk to the crest of the hill provides an extensive view of the great limestone expanse and, in season, the typical Burren flowers, such as bloody cranesbill, dense-flowered orchid, and spring gentian.

Parknabinnia II. About ³/₁₀ mile farther along the same byroad another signpost (**Leaba: Wedge Tomb**) W of the road points across a field (with foundations of a house unfinished in 1998) to a wedge grave almost entirely hidden in a hedge. From the stile beside the signpost a path leads directly to where a heap of stones indicates the entrance to the tomb. An enormous capstone rests on two sidestones with a large closing stone at the rear. The tomb is free from brambles and can easily be entered.

Parknabinnia III.
About 1⅕ miles farther along the same byroad is a third wedge grave, more complex in structure than the first two. Passing three houses, one to the left, two to the right of the byroad, and crossing the intersection with the Green Road (signposted), proceed to another **Leaba** sign, W of the road. Cross the roadside wall by the stile next to the signpost, bear right through a field, and proceed by a fairly well-trodden path about ⅒ mile, negotiating gaps in two stone walls at right angles to the road. The tomb is just beyond the second wall. It has traces of a cairn on the capstone, excellent doublewalling, and what looks like a court in front of the entrance, which is closed by a very tall slab at the S end.

Poulaphuca Wedge Grave. Heading S into the Burren from Bell Harbour towards Turlough, Carron, and Kilnaboy, look for third byroad to the right (W) and find remains of a signpost, well hidden

among a cluster of hazels and partially denuded of its original marker (**Leaba: Wedge Grave**). Of two tracks, take the one to the left and follow it (on foot) about ¾ mile uphill to a second Leaba marker, which points over the stone wall to the right (N). The tomb is a few yards from the wall, parallel to the road, a perfect specimen of the typical Burren wedge grave, rectangular, constructed of regular limestone slabs, without court or portico, closed at the E end by a stone with one corner broken off. Glorious views over the Burren all the way to Galway Bay. Poulaphuca means Hole (or Cave) of the Pooka (Demon or Fairy).

Teergonean Court Cairn *(facing page, bottom)*. Roadford, just N of Doolin. From post office take farm lane leading W towards the sea. After a little over a mile go through barred gate at end of lane. The tomb stands about 200 meters farther, with the sandy shore of Inisheer visible across the water. Uprights to the N define the court, with ruined chamber to the S. No capstone. Proximity to the shore and the view of Inisheer lend charm to this dilapidated site. The name of the townland, Teergonean, means Land without Birds.

Tulla Wedge Grave ("Mr. Malone's Wedge"/"Vartan's Folly"). From the S edge of Ennis turn E off Limerick-Galway road (N18) onto road (R352) marked Tulla. (A petrol station is a convenient marker for the turn.)

Proceed 8¾ miles to a crossroad where signs point ahead to Tulla and Scariff. Turn left onto a narrow, winding byroad and travel about 1½ miles to a junction. Continue on same byroad. Beyond second gate past junction, in field to right of road, the tomb is easily visible (possibly surrounded by cows). A small, neat affair, like the Burren wedge graves, it is comprised of four large stones: two long sidestones, a capstone with some of the cairn still remaining, and a fourth stone closing the chamber on the W end.

The neighborhood of Ennis is rich in antiquities, including Magh Adair, the inauguration place of Brian Boru and other Kings of Thomond (3¾ miles SW of Tulla), and the vast stone fort of Moghane near Dromoland Castle. Near Magh Adair is Quin Abbey (Franciscan), whose graveyard contains interesting epitaphs.

County Donegal

*C*ounty Donegal offers court cairns, wedge graves, and portal dolmens, as well as one of the biggest stone circles in Ireland. Non-megalithic treasures are the many cross slabs, especially on the Inishowen Peninsula (Fahan, Carndonagh), and the great stone fort, the Grianan of Ailech (Palace of the Sun), whose shape is mirrored in the modern church of St. Aengus at the foot of Greenan Mountain.

Ardmore Standing Stone. On E side of Inishowen peninsula about 1 mile NNE of Muff on road to Moville, take second turning to W, beside former Gillespie cottage. Drive up road to Y junction, turn right, pass two houses on left of road, continue past grove of trees to McDaid farm (total distance from main road ½ mile). Behind farmhouse is massive, squared-off stone, 6 feet tall, 3 feet wide, decorated on SE face with about 40 cupmarks, many with surrounding rings, a treasure of Bronze Age art. Extensive view over Lough Foyle.

Beltany Stone Circle *(facing page, top).* South of Raphoe (on R236) on Tops Hill. From town square of Raphoe follow signs for Beltany Stone Circle to agriculture center (about 1¼ miles). Outside gate to center leave car, turn right and follow lane uphill about ¼ mile to wooden stile, which gives access to fenced-in field, where on hilltop 64 stones averaging 4 feet in height remain of a circle, about

50 yards in diameter, which may have surrounded a cairn. (The interior of the circle is much disturbed.) Two "gates" - pairs of unusually tall orthostats, the tallest about 9 feet high - face each other on opposite sides (E and W). From the pair on the W, facing SE, you are in line with an outlier over 60 feet distant, a standing stone over 6 feet high. The name Beltany recalls Beltane, the Celtic May Day, and astronomical orientations at sunrise on May 1 have been suggested between the tallest pillar on the SW of the circle and a triangular, cupmarked stone 4½ feet tall aligned with it on the NE.

Gortnavern Portal Dolmen. Signposted on road from Kerrykeel (or Carrowkeel) to Rathmelton, about 1 mile S of Kerrykeel, W of Burnside River and about ¼ mile E of Kerrykeel-Rathmelton road. From second signpost (at foot of byroad) walk uphill on farm track.

About ¼ mile from farmhouse at foot of hill, enter second gate to right of track. Cross field and ford small stream. The dolmen is just beyond the rise at the top of the bank. A capstone 33 feet long by 7 feet wide, with possible cupmarks on the upper surface, rests on five slabs. The two portal stones are about 6 feet tall.

Kilclooney More Portal Dolmens.
Leaving Ardara on the R261 (towards Portnoo) go about 4 miles to Kilclooney church to the right (E) of the road. Turn onto byroad past church (and former

pub next door), then sharp right into lane leading to cottages. Passing cottages, follow lane between boggy fields, less than ½ mile, and through gate across lane. To the right are two portal dolmens, large and small, both facing E, with vestiges of cairn about 25 yards long. The larger tomb (to the E) has a capstone 20 feet long resting on portal stones 6 feet tall with a low sill between them. In profile it resembles a bird about to take flight. The smaller tomb to the W has one portal stone, low sill, two sidestones, and horizontal stone on top. Kilclooney More means Church of the Big Meadow.

Malin More Portal Dolmens *(below)* **and Full-Court Cairn** *(facing page)*. In the far SW corner of Donegal, 2½ miles beyond the exten-

sive and intricate complex of megalithic remains at Glencolumbcille (12 miles WNW of Killybegs), S of a byroad is a remarkable line of six portal dolmens, which may once have been covered by a single long cairn, fully 300 feet in length. The tombs at either end are oriented E-W, the four smaller ones N-S. The westernmost tomb has two capstones and massive orthostats 10 feet tall. Both it and the eastern-most tomb were partially reconstructed many years ago.

The neighborhood is rich in megalithic remains, the most arresting a (partially reconstructed) court cairn known as **Cloghanmore** (Big Stone Heap), about ½ mile to the E. It is 130 feet long with an oval court, 46 feet by 33 feet, from which open off (to the W) two parallel galleries, each with two chambers. Two single chambers open off the E end of the court on either side of the E-facing entrance, which is a passage over 9 feet long, lined by large orthostats. Each of the single chambers has an orthostat on the right of the entrance bearing curvilinear carvings, unique in court tombs, but associated with passage graves. For detailed descriptions of these megaliths and related monuments in the district consult *Glencolumbkille,* by Michael Herity (Dublin, 1980), available locally.

County Galway

*C*ounty Galway, *though rich in early churches, round towers, and Romanesque remains, has few accessible megaliths. The one described here is beautifully sited.*

Cleggan Court Cairn. From N59 (going S from Letterfrack towards Moyard) take first road leading W to Cleggan Pier (signposted for Inisbofin), and after about 4 miles turn off onto drive (on N side of road) leading to Cleggan Farm Holiday Cottages. Follow drive as far as farmhouse. From farmyard walk up lane through three gates. Turn left after third gate and go downhill (alongside stone wall and then fence) to where the tomb stands beside a low cliff on the N shore of Cleggan Bay. The court is gone, but a neat three-chambered gallery survives, with a capstone measuring about 10 feet sur-

mounting the second chamber. Both the tomb itself and the view over the sea, looking out towards Inisbofin and Inishark, are singularly satisfying.

Loughrea. In this area two objects of stone, neither of them mega-lithic, deserve a visit. World famous is the **Turoe Stone** *(facing page)*, a magnificent example of LaTène (Celtic) relief carving on a phallic boulder, now standing on a cattle grid in a field at Bullaun about 4 miles NNE of Loughrea. Abstract motifs (spirals, circles,curves) decorate the upper part of the 3 foot tall boulder, with a Greek key pattern below.

On the outskirts of Loughrea, close to the end of the N66 leading into Loughrea from Gort, look for a carved head of uncertain date, affixed to a wall near a public convenience. Locally called **Stoney Brennan** *(below),* it recalls the Celtic tradition of the severed head and sometimes wears a wreath suggesting continued veneration of ancient rituals.

On the same road, closer to Gort, stands **Thoor Ballylee**, which no lover of the poetry of W.B. Yeats will wish to miss.

County Kerry

*C**ounty Kerry, especially on the Dingle and Iveragh Peninsulas, has
such a wealth of megalithic and other stone monuments that the
following suggestions represent only a fraction of its treasures. In addi-
tion, promontory and inland forts, beehive huts of various dates, the
Gallarus Oratory, the collection of ogham stones near Dunloe Castle,
stone circles and alignments, and above all the monastic settlement on
Skellig Michael should not be overlooked. An excellent guidebook is*
Discovering Kerry *by T.J. Barrington (Dublin, 1976). For Dingle
Peninsula consult Maurice Sheehy,* Walks of Discovery in the Dingle
Peninsula *(1982). Stained glass windows by Harry Clarke (1889-1931),
Ireland's greatest artist in this medium, may be seen at the Presentation
Convent in Dingle and the Franciscan Friary in Killarney.*

Lissyvigeen Stone Circle. Leaving Killarney on N22 for Cork, after
about 2 miles turn left at byroad marked Iona Joinery. After about ⅕
mile on this road, walk about 50 paces up a lane to the left. Through
gate on left enter front yard of cottage. From rear of cottage cross

field to strip of woods, beyond which are circle and outliers. The circle is small (diameter about 14 feet) with only seven stones, about 4 feet tall, surrounded by an earthen bank 50 feet in diameter. The taller of the two standing stones (about 35 feet to the S) is 11 feet tall and has markings of dubious antiquity.

Dingle Peninsula

Caherard Wedge Grave (Grave of the Munsterman). About ½ mile NE of Ventry. Turning off main road from Dingle to Slea Head and Dunquin at sign for Ventry post office, go uphill a short distance and where road comes to dead end turn left on E-W road leading to Maumanorig. After about ⅕ mile leave road at disused quarry on right and take overgrown path on left side of quarry uphill. From top of quarry a stone wall runs uphill, passing a second

quarry and intersecting with a second stone wall. Climbing over the second wall, continue uphill towards ridge. First wall ends at intersection with third wall. About ¼ mile farther uphill and about ¼ mile below the crest is the grave, on SE side of hill. It is about 13 feet long and 3 feet wide. The chamber faces W. There is double-walling on the long sides, and there are three capstones, one tilted exuberantly in the air. The view from the site is worth the difficulty of finding this well-hidden tomb. Caherard means High Stone Fort.

Kilmalkedar Monastic Site. 4½ miles NW of
Dingle town on road towards Smerwick
Harbor, past Gallarus Oratory. Twelfth-century
Romanesque church containing alphabet
stone (cross-inscribed pillar with Roman lettering along edge). Outside are an ogham
stone pierced with a hole, three crosses, and a
sundial with spiral pattern.

In the same neighborhood (¾ mile W of Lateevemore and ¾ mile SE of Ballyferriter) at **Reask** *(right)* is a singularly satisfying example of a standing stone inscribed with a cross within a circle and adorned with an elegant elongated spiral design. Note the letters DNE (= Domine) to the left of the spiral and a notch on one side through which lovers could join their fingers.

Mam na hAltora (The Pass of the Altar) Wedge Grave *(below)*. On N86 going N from Anascaul towards Camp, just beyond road sign N86/0123, turn right onto byroad leading ultimately to Beehenagh. To right of byroad, about ⅛ mile from N86, a gate in the fence leads to a grassy path running downhill to the wedge grave (easily visible from gate). It has two capstones and very broad double-walling. Nearby are remains of another wedge grave and a holy well. To rear of first house on left of byroad is a poorly preserved wedge grave with displaced capstone, which has cupmarks. Just visible from the fence along the byroad, it can be approached by a track to the right of the farmhouse, but the householder discourages visitors.

If travelling SW from Camp on N86, ignore first byroad to left (F.), continue to top of rise (about 3 miles from Camp) and turn left on second byroad, described above.

Pookauncorrin (Doonmanagh) Wedge Grave. From N86 at Garrynadur (about 5 miles E of Dingle town) take road S (across from O'Sullivan's Bar) for about 50 yards. Turn left at junction, go uphill for about ¼ mile to Y junction with first sign for Kavanagh Quarries, turn right and follow road toward Doonties about ⅕ mile to second Quarries sign. Turn right onto side road (with house on left), go uphill about ½ mile to Quarries, continue another ⅖ mile past a pump house and a radio transmitter (both to right of road), to where a boreen leads off to the left with ample space for parking at the entrance. Walk down the boreen, passing a gate into a cowpasture on the right, continue to second gate, also to right of boreen, and entering through this gate go uphill on cowpath inside stone wall. Passing through a gap in a second stone wall, at right angles to the first, you will see the grave on the crest of the hill, overlooking Doonties. Some stones of original cairn can be seen built into wind-break at right angles to grave, possibly to afford shelter to sheep, which sometimes occupy the chamber. Total distance from head of boreen to grave is only about ¼ mile, but this is one of the best-hidden megaliths. Spectacular views over Dingle Bay to Iveragh Peninsula and SE to the Reeks of Macgillycuddy.

Graigue Standing Stone. Returning by same route, after passing Quarries, note in field to left a standing stone split vertically. The most prominent object along this road is the radio transmitter on the hilltop. Looking SW across the road from here, one can see the hilltop on which Pookauncorrin is located.

Iveragh Peninsula (Ring of Kerry)

Coom Wedge Grave. From Portmagee on road leading to St. Finan's Bay and Ballinskelligs, proceed almost eight miles (passing St. Finan's Bay) and, about 2 miles NW of Ballinskelligs, turn off on farm track to the right (just before a small group of houses). Down this track, in a field to the left, clearly visible from the top of the hill, is the wedge grave. The field is easy to enter, but cattle will probably be grazing and care should be taken to close gates. The capstone over the main chamber is about 10 feet long, there is a roofless portico, and some of the slabs are about 4 feet high.

Eightercua Alignment. About 1 mile SSE of Waterville on the N70, on a ridge E of the road, is an alignment of four standing stones, the tallest about 10 feet high, running E-W for about 30 feet. Easily seen from the road. There are traces of a cairn nearby, connected with a slab running S from one of the standing stones.

County Limerick

C *ounty Limerick has at one easily accessible site some of the very few surviving remains of houses dating from Neolithic times, as well as a wealth of other prehistoric remains, including stone circles, tombs, standing stones, and crannogs (artificial islands constructed to support dwellings).*

Lough Gur Stone Circles *(below)* **and Wedge Grave** *(next page)*. Just E of T50A (Limerick-Bruff), 12 miles SSE of Limerick, 2½ miles N of Bruff, signposted and approached by a stile, is the **Lios** (Circular Fort), the largest stone circle in Ireland, 150 feet in diameter, with a contiguous row of more than one hundred uprights, the tallest almost 9 feet. One huge stone, perhaps twenty tons in weight, stands on the NE side of the circle. The entrance on the E is flanked by two stones, one over 6 feet high, the other over 7 feet, one flat-topped, the other pointed (like the "female" and "male" standing stones found in Donegal and elsewhere). An earthen bank thirty feet wide,

now overgrown with trees, surrounds the entire ring on the outside. About 130 yards to the NE is a smaller circle, cut off by a fence from the Lios.

Beside the byroad running from Holycross (S of Bruff) along the S shore of Lough Gur (leading to a standing stone at Lough Gur Cross, ¾ mile farther E, and an Information Center at the far end of the Lough) is a wedge grave (signposted and approached by a stile) just E of the byroad. The grave is 29 feet long by 21 feet wide and has a covered gallery with a smaller chamber at the SW end, also with capstone, double-walling, and many traces of stones from surrounding cairn.

On same side of byroad, closer to Bruff-Limerick road and not signposted, is a second wedge grave in poor condition, known as Leaba na Muice (the Pig's Bed). The whole area around Lough Gur invites exploration. Nearby at Bruree is the DeValera Museum, rich in mementoes of the late President of the Republic, born in New York, but brought up at Bruree.

County Mayo

ounty Mayo is the jewel of the West for megalith-lovers, because of the number and variety of its monuments, set in glorious contexts of sea and mountain. The megalithic sites mentioned here constitute only a fraction of Mayo's abundance. Not to be missed is the exemplary and beautiful Visitor Center at Céide Fields. Mayo is also rich in the magnificent stained glass windows by Harry Clarke (1889–1931). St. Patrick's Church at Newport, with Clarke's Last Judgment, is convenient for visitors to Achill Island.

Ballyglass Center-Court Cairn. Leaving Ballycastle on R314 (W towards Behy, Belderrig, and Belmullet), turn left (S) after about ⅕ mile onto byroad signposted for Ballyglass. At first crossroad turn right and proceed to fork, at which take road to right. At third house on left, property of Mr. and Mrs. Patrick Grehan, ask permission to view the tomb. (A small number of visitors at a time, who promise to close gates, are usually welcome.) If permitted, enter through farm gate to right of house, go through second gate, follow path straight ahead into pasture, where the tomb, nearly 30 yards long, will be immediately visible. Although much overgrown, its structure is unmistakable: an oval center court about 40 feet long, with an

entrance on the NE, and two double-chambered galleries facing each other across the court, one with lintel stone in place. Capstones from each gallery tilt down into court.

The site of an earlier Neolithic dwelling lies beneath part of this tomb, probably related to the settlement at Céide Fields about 4 miles W. During excavation of the court tomb in 1969 post holes and a trench led to the discovery of the site of the house, fully excavated in 1971. A reconstruction may be seen at Céide Fields.

About 250 yards to the S is a full-court tomb with an oval court and two- or three-chambered gallery. It has a false entrance on the N. Twenty-eight court tombs are known in the neighborhood of Ballycastle, near Buntrahir Bay, which may have been the original landing place of the builders.

Breastagh Ogham Stone/Rathfran Park Wedge Grave/St. Patrick's Stone/Carbad More Court Cairn. Follow R314 from Killala towards Ballycastle, but after Palmerstown Bridge turn immediately off to right (N) on road signposted for **Breastagh Ogham Stone**. About 1 mile from Bridge on right (E) side of road, just over stone wall (cross by stile), is grave, signposted **Caislean Cuirt Rathfran Dolmen**, with gallery about 10 feet long and 6 feet wide. There are four tall stones on the S side, four on the N, and the entrance is marked by two jambstones. Double-walling is visible at the E end, where stones from a nearby (destroyed) circle are piled. The grave is considerably overgrown. In the distance the ruins of Rathfran "Abbey" (13th-century Dominican priory) are visible, beautifully situated on a tidal inlet of Killala Bay, where seabirds are abundant.

On same road, about ½ mile farther towards Kilcummin Strand, is **Breastagh Ogham Stone** (signposted). Access to field (W of road) is over stile. The stone, square in section, is more than 7 feet tall and is inscribed in ogham lettering along one edge. A historical marker transliterates the inscription and suggests that the stone is a reused menhir.

It is well worth continuing along this road to Kilcummin Strand, where the French landed in 1798, to see the tiny ruined church and the grave of St. Cummin with related pillarstones and slabs; but beyond Rathfran and Breastagh, before following road to the right towards Kilcummin, go straight ahead a short distance (a total of about 3½ miles from Palmerstown Bridge) to Foghill, where to the right (E) of the road stands a pillarstone,

reputedly set up by St. Patrick, who brought Christianity to this area and founded the original church at Killala, its location still marked by a round tower. **St. Patrick's Stone** stands by itself in a field overlooking Lacken Bay, whose shallow waters wash Lacken Strand, one

of the loveliest beaches on the mostly deserted coast of North Mayo, a magical land- and seascape from here to Belmullet in the far West.

On the way back to Palmerstown Bridge it is just worth looking for remains of a double-court cairn at **Carbad More** (1 mile S of Breastagh, W of road and close to it). It is possible to make out two courts, at either end of the cairn, each leading to a gallery.

Carrowcrom Wedge Grave *(below)*. From Bonniconlon (about 4½ miles ESE of Ballina on R294) take first road to right (SW, towards Attymass) after entering town from W. Follow road about 2 miles, passing Oatlands House on left and cemetery on right. Ignore first two paved byroads leading off to right (NW), but at third byroad turn left off Bonniconlon-Attymass road. In field at angle of these two roads, not far from corner, is the wedge grave, a beautiful specimen of its kind. The capstone is almost 7 feet long, and much of the cairn is preserved towards the rear. There are four orthostats at the front, facing SW, and three large sidestones to the left of the entrance, two on the right, defining the gallery. The double-walling characteristic of wedge graves is easily visible. The field can be entered by a stile opposite the grave or by a gate about ⅒ mile from the intersection of the two roads. (Be sure to close the gate securely, since cattle are usually in the field.) Carrowcrom means Crooked Quarter.

Carrowkilleen Court Cairns *(facing page)*. Three miles from the out-skirts of Crossmolina on road to Belmullet (N59), S of road, is farm of Mr. and Mrs. John V. Keane. With their permission, enter property by path to right of cottage, leading back to gate into fenced paddock. A gap in the fence leads into a pasture, where a cairn about 185 feet long lies to the left, partly concealing what may have been three sep-

arate tombs, aligned along an E-W axis. Farthest to the E is a court opening into a two-chambered gallery. W of this is another court with a side-chamber leading off to the S from its first chamber. Still farther W is a three-chambered gallery with what may be a forecourt facing W. Carrowkilleen is the largest complex of court tombs in Ireland. The word "killeen" refers to an early monastic site used as a burial place for unbaptized children.

Dolmen of the Four Maols *(next page)*. Leaving Ballina on L134, S to Castlebar, just before railroad station on edge of town, a signpost on right side of road reads **Tuamba Maighiotoct: Dolmen of the Four Maols 1 km.** Turn right and follow byroad to point where on left another signpost, now deprived of its sign, still marks the spot where a stile leads over a wall at the foot of a steep incline. Over the stile turn right, take well-defined path uphill, and the dolmen looms

on the ridge. Its capstone rests on three orthostats, with a fourth a short distance away. Curious cattle or sheep may investigate the visitor. The name derives from the legend that four brothers named Maol were hanged on this spot for murdering their teacher, Ceallach, Bishop of Kilmoremoy.

Drumgollach Court Cairn *(facing page, top)*. From N59 between Bangor and Mulranny (about 11 miles S of Bangor, 8 N of Mulranny) take byroad to W, signposted for Castlehill. Proceed about $\frac{1}{10}$ mile (passing ruined church some distance N of byroad) and at second track leading off byroad to right (N) go up very steep hill, passing grove of trees on right of track, and after 1 mile approach McManamon farm, also on right. Gate leads to driveway going downhill to farmhouse. To right of house, in field of tall grass often used by cattle, is the cairn. At end closer to house an antechamber leads to a gallery entered between two tall jambstones and closed at rear by large septal stone. Two stones lying on either side of entrance may be fallen lintel stones. The chamber farthest from the house is covered by a capstone over 9 feet long by 6 feet wide, with cupmarks on the surface. The McManamons were notable for their friendly welcome and their pride in their prehistoric monument. Since the death

of Mrs. McManamon in 1995 the caretaker has been equally welcoming. Views towards Achill Island and back towards the Nephin Beg range are extraordinary.

Slievemore (Achill Island) Full-Court Cairn *(below)*. From Keel on Achill take road (N) signposted to Deserted Village and McDowell's Hotel, passing on right Minaun View Bar (on E edge of Keel). Proceed about $1\frac{1}{10}$ miles, crossing two small bridges, and take first paved road to right (signposted for McDowell's). After another

$^7/_{10}$ mile a signpost on right of road, reading **Megalithic Tomb**, points across road to left. Here stile gives access over stone wall to steep overgrown lane between wire fences. A climb of slightly less than $^1/_2$ mile leads to the cairn. You will pass one house (over fence to right of path) and come to second stone wall with second stile. From this point the cairn is clearly visible a little farther uphill. The chamber with capstone is on the downhill side of the tomb; uphill is another chamber whose stones are tumbled. Beyond lies a circular court 15 feet in diameter. The view to the S over Achill to the sea is spectacular. While on Achill do not miss the superb strand at Keem, where basking sharks are sometimes sighted. Slievemore means Big Mountain.

Srahwee (Altar) Wedge Grave. From L100 (T334) between Louisburgh and Leenane, about 6 miles S of Louisburgh, turn W on byroad to Killadoon and proceed about 2 miles, crossing Carrownisky River. Just N of road, across from Lough Nahaltora and W of a farmhouse, is grave. Facing W, it exhibits all the characteristics of a wedge grave: tapered form, double-walling, septal slab, large capstone with traces of cairn, partially covering

gallery about 13 feet long. Used as a Mass Rock in penal days, it gave its name (Altar) to the nearby lake.

County Roscommon

*C*ounty Roscommon is included here because of the proximity to the Mayo border of one splendid megalith, easily accessible and belonging to the category of portal dolmen, relatively rare in this area.

Drumanone Portal Dolmen. About 2 miles W of Boyle on road to Tubbercurry (N294), signposted, N of road (across from gateway into wooded area). Parking space is available by house on N side of road. An easy path leads a short distance uphill to the tracks of the Sligo-Mullingar railway, on either side of which is a gate (be sure to close). Beyond second gate, immediately to left of path, is opening into pasture, where the dolmen stands a few yards away. Between two portal stones, each over 8 feet tall, a huge doorstone completely closes the entrance, which faces NE. Single stones comprise the sides. The capstone (about 15 feet by 12½ feet) has slid back and now touches the ground. Stones from a cairn are scattered nearby. Cattle, which usually occupy the field, seem used to visitors.

County Sligo

*C*ounty Sligo holds two of the greatest passage grave cemeteries in Ireland, as well as textbook examples of the court cairn type and a few notable portal tombs. It also holds, at Drumcliffe, the grave of W.B. Yeats "under bare Benbulben's head" and innumerable sites mentioned in his poetry, as well as recognizable backgrounds for some paintings of horseracing on the strand by Jack Yeats.

Carrowkeel Megalithic Cemetery. From N4 (Dublin-Sligo) take byroad W at Castlebaldwin, signposted **Carrowkeel Passage Tombs 6 km**. (There are seven signposts along the twisting route.) After the sixth sign is a gate, beyond which the track is exceedingly rough, though still passable by car. About ⁷⁄₁₀ mile beyond a second gate a cliff rises to the right, where a very steep climb through treacherous brambles and heather leads to the two most spectacular cairns, E

and F (not signposted and easy to miss). Cairn E, which combines features of court cairn and passage grave, is 120 feet long and 8 feet tall. It has a forecourt to the S, no gallery, but a huge slab12 feet long blocking off a cruciform chamber. To the N a passage grave opens onto the end of the cairn. Cairn F has two transepts and a corbelled roof. Farther along the road and well marked is parking area, from which a steep overgrown path leads uphill to four tombs (G, H, K, L) the farthest about ½ mile from base of hill. G and K are notable for their cruciform chambers and double lintels at the entrance. There are many other megalithic remains in this great cemetery, which should be explored with caution because of the treacherous footing and the fragility of some of their limestone components. Despite such cautions, the effort to visit these cairns is repaid, not only by the intrinsic interest of the tombs themselves, but because of the glorious views from the summit of the ridges of the Bricklieve Mountains on which they stand - over Lough Arrow to the E and all the way to Knocknarea to the N. Carrowkeel means Narrow Quarter.

Carrowmore Megalithic Cemetery. About 2 miles SW of Sligo town, amply signposted and dominated by a Visitors' Center, where guidance can be obtained for visits to the many megalithic sites in the area. From N4 (Dublin-Sligo) turn off on byroad to W (opposite

Carraroe Schoolhouse). Take second left and at T-junction turn right. At second T-junction turn left and proceed to Visitors' Center, across road from McGarry Riding Stables. About thirty megalithic structures, many of them close to the road and easily inspected, remain from an estimated two hundred, most of which were destroyed by quarrying and landclearance. Excavations by Swedish archaeologists beginning in 1977 suggest that the tombs were built between c. 4800 B.C. and c. 3800 B.C. and were reused until the Iron Age. Of the many monuments worth visiting the most impressive is Tomb 7, dated by the excavators to c. 4200 B.C., and consisting of a polygonal central chamber surrounded by a boulder circle. It is oriented towards the still-unexcavated cairn atop the hill of Knocknarea, known as Miosgan Meadhbha, "Maeve's Lump." The cairn is over 35 feet high and 200 in diameter, surrounded by smaller cairns. It is an exhilarating experience to climb to the top of Knocknarea (1083 feet), and this can be done easily by a path (signposted) starting at Grange North. The Visitors' Center can supply brochures and an excellent illustrated guidebook by the head of the Swedish excavation team, who notes that the Carrowmore tombs lack the passage normal in Irish passage graves and can be linked with the passage grave tradition only by the grouping in a cemetery and the finding of passage tomb artifacts in some of them. Carrowmore means Great Quarter.

Creevykeel Full-Court Cairn. On N15 (Sligo-Bundoran), 1½ miles NE of Cliffoney, just E of road, signposted and almost too easy of

access. Excavated by Harvard Archaeological Mission in 1935, this is one of the largest and most comprehensible court cairns, its structure grasped at a glance, its components free of overgrowth. A wedge-shaped cairn about 200 feet long faces E, where an entrance leads W to an open court, about 30 by 50 feet. To W of court a gallery about 30 feet long with two chambers leads still farther W to three single-chambered tombs, with entrances on the long sides of the cairn. At entrance to gallery are orthostats 6 feet high. In NW part of court are remains of a kiln dating from the early Christian period. Creevykeel means Narrow Branchy Place.

Deerpark (Magheraghanrush) Center-Court Cairn. Leaving Sligo on road to Leckaun, take N16 (for Enniskillen) only to junction just beyond hospital (on right of road). Here take road straight ahead (not N16, which continues to left). Almost at once road forks; take lefthand road (for Manorhamilton) and go about 4 miles E, past Colgagh Lough (on right of road). At left of road two signs read **Machavie Chon Rus/Deerpark Court Tomb**, and **Giant's Grave**. To right of road (S) an upaved track leads uphill about a mile to the site, on the summit of a limestone ridge overlooking Lough Gill and Colgagh Lough. The tomb is about 100 feet in length, the center court about 50 feet long with entrance on S. From it two galleries open off the E end, one off the W. All are two-chambered, and one of the E galleries has a broken lintel stone, still precariously in place. In the immediate

neighborhood are other remains, including a stone circle (signposted) off the path leading to the court cairn.

Tawnatruffaun Portal Dolmen (The Giant's Griddle). About 5 miles SW of Dromore West. On N59 (going from Ballina towards Sligo) cross bridge over Easky River (about 11 miles from Ballina); take byroad to right (S) and continue about 2⅕ miles to "Yield" sign. Here turn right and shortly cross Buncroney River. Proceed until you see a cottage to right of road. To left of road, about 50 yards back, cross very boggy fields to reach stone wall, into which the tomb has been incorporated. It has a slightly tilted capstone over 6 feet long, resting on two portal stones, with a third serving as backstone. The sidestones survive only on the side away from the wall, and the interior of the chamber is thus exposed. The isolation and the difficulty of finding the dolmen add to its tremendous charm, as does the superb view of the Ox Mountains in the distance to the SE. Still more difficult to find (local guidance suggested) are the two **Griddles of the Fiana** (the **Great Griddle,** a gallery grave, the **Small Griddle** *(inset),* a wedge grave) about 2 miles away to the SW, on the other side of the Easky River.